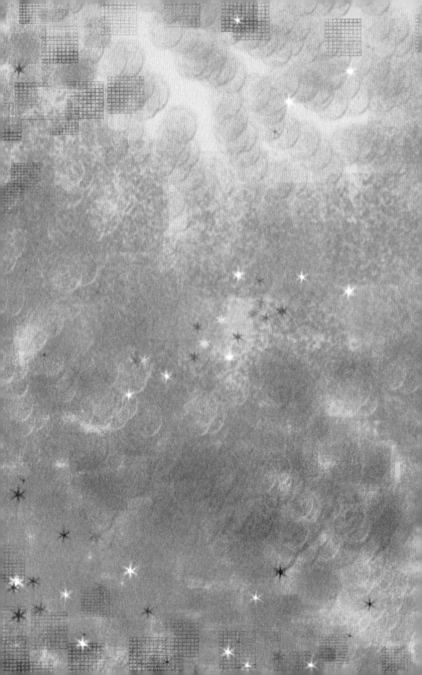

Imagine yourself as anything
you want to be, and let your
spiritual nature lead you to victory.
When times are tough, don't give up.
God hears your prayers,
and He will answer them.

— Donna Fargo

It is with deepest devotion that I dedicate this book to my sweetheart and soul mate, the most unique and thoughtful person I've ever known, the love of my life, Stan Silver. He liked to stay in the background, but he was my rock, my superman, who was and always will be in the foreground of my heart.

Blue Mountain Arts, Inc.
P.O. Box 4549, Boulder, Colorado 80306

Everything Is Possible with God

Is Possible with

God

You Are Strong,
and the Best Is Yet
to Come

Donna Fargo

Blue Mountain Press™
Boulder, Colorado

Everything Is Possible with God

Dare to dream. Open your heart, and let yourself go as far as your mind will take you. Drop any regrets and negative thoughts that hold you down. Recognize your talents. Be thankful for what makes you *you*.

Imagine yourself as anything you want to be, and let your spiritual nature lead you to victory. When times are tough, don't give up. You are more than enough. God doesn't make mistakes. He hears your prayers, and He will answer them. He has not lost your message or forgotten you.

Count your blessings; love your life; treasure your family and friends and all that you're thankful for. Above all, remember that... everything is possible with God.

You Are Stronger Than You May Realize

You're strong like a beautiful tree in the forest. You have experienced the winds of change and challenge, and you are still standing. Like enduring roots reaching down into the earth, your foundation of faith and spirituality will keep you firmly planted.

When you've done all you think you can, stay determined. When you're doubtful and frustrated, don't despair. When you can't see tomorrow, just get through today.

Honor your heart's direction. Stand your ground. Storms and the weather made that big tree strong, and it's still standing, too, just like you.

In the feelings that you keep to yourself, you may sometimes have questions. Guard your confidence and promise yourself that you were born to win and not lose, and with God's help, you will be empowered mightily.

How to Live
a Fulfilled Life

Wrap your arms around life and be the
   exceptional person you are meant to be

Understand that you're not alone and lots of
   people are praying for you

Block out any negative chatter and only listen to
   the positive voices within you

Value your resilience and keep your integrity

Be your own advocate and treasure your unique
   qualities and great potential

Live your life in a spirit of cooperation
   with others

Be someone who thinks outside limitations
    when you know you need to make a change

Know that attitude is a choice and you can win
    any battle

Remember that fear must have your permission
    to occupy your mind

Believe in miracles and realize that God is
    on your side

Trust that all things are possible (and there are
    no exceptions) if you can only believe

If You Don't Choose Your Thoughts, Your Thoughts Will Choose You

Thoughts can help or hinder you,
but you can control what you think and do.
If you just let any old thoughts roam freely,
some of them can unnecessarily hurt you.
But you don't need to entertain them.
You can choose what you say and do.

Line up your thoughts with your words
    and actions
and it won't be long until you'll find
that wishes live in your heart
and doubts come from the mind.
Sometimes you need to doubt your doubts
and choose your thoughts and decide
if they're a friend or an enemy to you.
For every action there's a consequence —
your destiny depends on what you say and do.
If you don't choose your thoughts,
your thoughts will choose you.

Whatever Your Age,
You Are Still a Child of God

Remember when you were a child and how easy it was to play pretend? You could get lost in your dreams and suspended in your imagination, and it seemed like you could do anything. You were the main character in your own movies of what you wanted to happen, and you'd go to that wonderland, that place where you were so happy that your dream had actually come true.

You may be grown-up now, but you are still a child of God — so why not believe you have that same power? Except this time, take your dreams to that higher place and declare with certainty: "I break the chain of habitual thinking of worst-case scenarios based on my physical being. I invite my imagination and God to create the realities I pray for in my life. I will appreciate every blessing and each bit of newfound wisdom that come to me." Then state your wants and needs clearly to God, thank Him for giving you the desires of your heart, and absolutely know they're on the way.

What's Holding You Back?

God said that all things are possible to those who believe. That means everything, anything, all. He didn't list any exceptions. He doesn't identify anyone specifically… except those who believe. And He wouldn't tell us to do something that we weren't able to do. That wouldn't be fair, and God is surely fair.

If you've been messing around just doing whatever, there's no better time than now to change. Since God's laws don't change… it's up to you to get the job done. You don't even have to understand it all. Believe without the evidence. That's God's way. That's what faith is. And faith gives you the power to achieve anything.

When you don't know what to do,
which way to turn, or whom to trust...
When you can't decide whether
one action would be better than another...
When you're anxious and confused
and your heart and mind are in conflict...
Don't forget to pray about it.

Prayer will bring you peace
and help you rest your case.
It will make you feel better.
God has told us not to worry or be afraid.
He wants us to cast our cares on Him —
so surrendering your problems
is really an act of obedience and devotion.

Remember that God is love.
He is faithful and He is good.
Pray about everything that concerns you...
and know without a doubt
that your prayers will be answered.

Life Is on Your Side, and God Is Too

When you're struggling with your faith and feelings, and discouragement has crowded out your hope, try to refocus and reclaim your power.

Erase the negatives and start over by thinking that life must be on your side because you're not defeated — you're alive! Take some time to be grateful for your blessings, and remember what you have and don't have and what you can do that perhaps some cannot. Don't forget that you're a spirit first and you have a body, mind, and soul to serve you.

Then believe in your heart and say aloud that God is on your side, too, just as He Himself has told you...

"Whatever you ask for in prayer, believe that you have received it, and it will be yours."

(Mark 11:24 NIV)

"For no word from God will ever fail."

(Luke 1:37 NIV)

Always remember that life is on your side...
and God is too.

Believe

When you're down, believe that this is just a place you're in and that you won't be discouraged forever. Think about this… it wouldn't make sense that God would challenge you to be an overcomer if you weren't able to be, so don't let this disappointment define you. This is just a battle — it's not the war. Besides, it may be a blessing in disguise.

Believe that clarity will come when you're ready to move forward. After you've done all you know to do, trust that God is working out the details so you can be blessed. Realize that there may be lessons you need to learn, and don't worry. Just know that your day will come in perfect timing.

When life's not fair, believe that it's still good. You can choose to be hopeful and faithful, no matter what you're experiencing, and you don't have to let anything steal your joy. You can still count some blessings that others may not have. Believe with all your being that God loves you. After all, He gave you your dreams, your vision, and your purpose — and since His spirit actually lives in your heart, how can you possibly fail?

Use These Keys to Help You Unlock Any Door

Faith… It is taking God at His word. It's the step beyond hope. It's God's gift to His children.

Optimism… It's trusting that you can do whatever you think you can.

Courage… It's the strength that comes to your rescue when you feel lost or dejected. It's the kind of bravery that will show you how to overcome disappointment and perform the impossible.

Willingness… Sometimes it's hard to believe that you can really have what you want, but with a willing mind, you can train your spirit to use its authority to help you reach your every goal.

Imagination… The child within you needs a fantasy place to escape to sometimes, where you are free to explore your creative spirit without preconceptions.

Truth… When you're honest with yourself and others, you can avoid misunderstandings and save yourself a lot of time.

Patience… Whether you possess it naturally or have to develop it, you need it. It's a quiet kind of confidence and a reward worth the wait.

Prayer… This is the great balancer. It's our direct line to God that connects us with His spirit. It is the key to His kingdom. It humbles us and keeps us strong.

Love… It's the greatest commandment: love God, everyone, and yourself. Faith works by it, and happiness is a result of it. Love makes your life more beautiful.

If you rely on these keys, they will give you the guidance you need to unlock any door.

If You're Having Trouble Helping Yourself, You're Not Alone

Sooner or later, many get to the place where there is no medicine for what they need and their only hope is God. Some may say they've asked God for help and their condition hasn't changed or maybe even gotten worse, so now what?

At times like this, it's important to remember that God is sovereign, and we're not, so we need Him. If we don't have a relationship with Him, we are working with only two-thirds of our potential because we're body, soul, AND spirit. And since God is a spirit and we're made in His image (spiritually), we probably need to communicate with Him in that way.

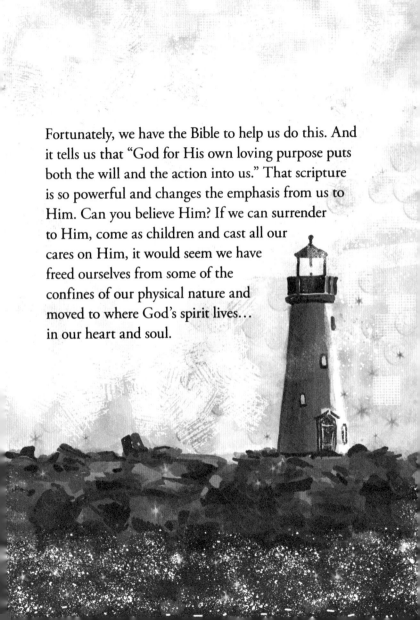

Fortunately, we have the Bible to help us do this. And it tells us that "God for His own loving purpose puts both the will and the action into us." That scripture is so powerful and changes the emphasis from us to Him. Can you believe Him? If we can surrender to Him, come as children and cast all our cares on Him, it would seem we have freed ourselves from some of the confines of our physical nature and moved to where God's spirit lives… in our heart and soul.

God's Got Your Back — You Will Not Fail!

The spirit of God lives inside you. He loves you because you're His own. Friends may desert you and families disown you, but He'll never leave you alone.

If you're broken, He'll fix you — after all, He created you. You are one of His dreams that came true. He'll answer your prayers — sometimes out of the blue — after He sees your faith in Him too. He promises an abundance of life here on earth, and — though it may sound odd — we're also blessed with the miraculous spiritual life everlasting. Just imagine! What a God!

The prisons we make for ourselves are no place for the forgiven who've made mistakes they're so sorry for. He even said we could cast ALL our cares on Him. You just can't out-love Him; He loves you so much more. He's a "hands-on" God. He'll give you the desires of your heart, make your dreams come true, and make you well. He's as good as His word if you will only believe Him… He's got your back and you will not fail!

Keep the Faith

Faith lives in your heart beside your dreams and wishes. It's not a myth. It's real, and it is the one thing that pleases God... and you, too, for that matter. It's that important. It's like breath to your desire; it's the momentum behind your potential. Its greatest fear is that you'll abandon it before it can help you out.

Hope is the step before faith, and faith requires it in order to be manifested. Hope wants you to be happy and satisfied, but hope is always in the future. Faith is always now. Hope is a wish for something someday; faith is believing you've got it now without seeing any evidence. The soul loves it, the mind requires it, and the spirit has to have it to possess what you're striving for.

Faith inspires confidence and brings the expectation of a positive outcome when you make an effort to believe and take action. It's the most comforting friend there is when you're sick or sad and especially when you're failing. Don't be caught without it. It's the possible in every dream and the bright light in your future. It can color every day beautiful and help you keep going when it seems like there's no end in sight.

Give It Away

When you're full of joy, give it away, and it will be returned to you when you need it. Share your smiles and hugs and words of encouragement, and feel the reflection of these sunny thoughts and feelings shining back on you. Remember that when you sow seeds of optimism in someone else's life, they will bloom for you, too, someday.

If you keep recalling painful or hurtful memories, realize that you're only punishing yourself. Don't get stuck on a treadmill in your mind that takes you round and round but gets you nowhere. Let that hurt go, just as you would untie a knot.

Sometimes, just changing what you call something changes your attitude toward it and makes it less burdensome. If Lady Luck has lost your number, give that bad luck away by changing its name to "opportunity." When there's no pot of gold on the horizon, go inside yourself and find the motivation, resolve, and self-esteem that you need to make progress.

See all the problems you don't have, and be thankful for the blessings you do have. Be grateful for your special qualities and for the grace by which you received them. Accept them with humility and share them freely. Tell Lady Luck you don't want that unlucky number anymore, so you're giving it back and getting ready for some good fortune.

Watch what you pay attention to. Focus on the solutions instead of the problems. Observe the thoughts that are binding you, and release them to the universe. Let love fill up your heart, and give it away.

You've Got Choices

When you have something particularly challenging to deal with, try to remind yourself…

You've got this moment… You can choose to be happy or unhappy. You can choose what you think, what you say, and how you feel. You can choose to be hopeful or hopeless, to respond angrily or cheerfully, to be bored or interested.

You've got this day… No matter what the weather is like — it's just weather. You can choose what kind of day it will be — beautiful or awful or somewhere in between. You can choose what you will do and what you won't — to give up or give in or go on. You have a choice to do something or nothing, to start now or later. You can choose your attitude about what you're facing.

You've got your life... If you're not happy, satisfied, encouraged, and hopeful, you're cheating yourself. You can talk and talk to yourself about what you need to do to honor your life, but if you don't turn those thoughts into actions, you're playing games and giving up to whatever comes to mind.

You've got the power to make choices... Your life is the manifestation of the choices you make each moment and each day. When you use this awesome gift to your best advantage, there is nothing you can't do.

The Ten Greatest Gifts
of Strong People

1. Strong people are true to themselves. They believe in their dreams and their purpose. They realize that they have the gift of emotional sense and intuition to create a vision for their lives.

2. They embrace the awesomeness of nature and know they are a part of something big. They know why they're here and what they're called to do.

3. They know they have a spirit, mind, and body, and they take responsibility for all three. They renew their minds with spiritual truths. They think positive thoughts, exercise, and maintain a healthy diet.

4. They appreciate people's differences, respect everyone's unique qualities, and accept people for who they are.

5. They treat others the way they wish to be treated. They are generous with their kind words and quick to forgive. They harbor no resentments and are sensitive to the harsh realities of the world.

6. When they're challenged, they know that they will not only survive but prosper. They learn from their mistakes and move on with grit and gratitude.

7. They use their strong feelings of joy, compassion, and love to build meaningful relationships. They remember that love never goes out of style and will never lose its importance.

8. They embrace the image of who they want to be and become the person no one else can be. They see themselves in full bloom.

9. They choose to be happy. They know that they have but one life to live, and they are determined to live it well.

10. In this fast-paced, ever-changing world, strong people choose to celebrate life every day by being the best example of who they are.

God Is with You All the Time

He's with you in the morning;
    He's with you in the night
He knows every tear-stained glass window
    of your soul
He loves you just the way you are
    even when you feel you are nothing
He knows the question and the answer
    and the way to reach your goal

He's with you on the mountaintops
    when everything is perfect
He's with you in the valleys
    when you have lost your way
He knows the fears that confound you
    and keep you from receiving
He sees the faith in all your efforts
    and hears every prayer you pray

He knows the thoughts that tiptoe barefoot
    along the banks of your heart
He's the landlord of your soul and your mind
He won't impose His will on you, but He'll help
    you make your own choices
When you struggle for the answers that you
    want so much to find

He made the wonders of the universe,
    the sun and moon and stars
The rain clouds and the water in the cool
    country stream
He's in your father and your mother and every
    good-luck four-leaf clover
He lives in your heart and knows every dream
    you dream

When you think you're alone in this place
    called life
Don't be afraid; God is with you all the time

You Are Strong, and the Best Is Yet to Come

You can do more than you think you can. Try to look at obstacles as lessons and see every goal as reachable. Even if your wings are a little damaged, you can still fly. You can still touch the sky. You can still make a rainbow. You can still dream. You can still try.

Don't let anyone take away your hope, get you down, or make you give up. Don't let anyone or anything steal your power. Stay strong, encouraged, and hopeful. Know that you are loved.

Wholeheartedly believe that everything is possible with God and that He really is as good as His word. See your faith as a powerful source guiding you through each day, and let it free your mind to make room for expanded awareness and new light.

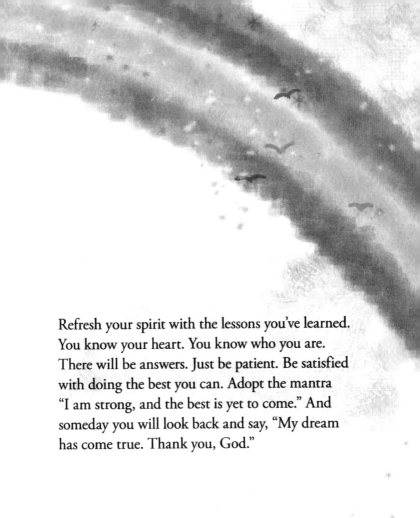

Refresh your spirit with the lessons you've learned.
You know your heart. You know who you are.
There will be answers. Just be patient. Be satisfied
with doing the best you can. Adopt the mantra
"I am strong, and the best is yet to come." And
someday you will look back and say, "My dream
has come true. Thank you, God."

May God Bless You

Bless you for being you. Bless you for inspiring others with your kindness and for caring enough to lift people up and accept them without judgment.

Bless you for your compassion, consistency, and understanding. You believe the best of others. You live your life by example and practice the Golden Rule.

Bless you for celebrating every triumph, for consoling and comforting and sharing the pain of those who hurt. There is no ill will in your heart, no room for selfishness or resentment. You guide and enlighten, and you bring out the good in others.

Bless you for your strength and perseverance. In the face of adversity, your courage embodies wisdom, humanity, dignity, and a spirit of inclusiveness.

Bless you for living your life so that people recognize God in you. After all, you're made in His image spiritually, so there should be a resemblance because you're one of His children. You have power and royalty within you, and you are in God's will if you claim your inheritance. Celebrate the gift of your life always.

May your rewards be great, and may all the love you give out be returned to you. May you continue to be a bright light of hope and positive energy in this crazy, mixed-up world.

May God's richest blessings be yours.

About the Author

With her first album, *The Happiest Girl in the Whole U.S.A.*, which achieved platinum status and earned her a Grammy, Donna Fargo established herself as an award-winning singer, songwriter, and performer. Her credits include seven Academy of Country Music awards, five Billboard awards, fifteen Broadcast Music Incorporated (BMI) writing awards, and two National Association of Recording Merchandisers awards for best-selling artist. She has also been honored by the Country Music Association, the National Academy of Recording Arts and Sciences, and the Music Operators of America, and she was the first inductee into the North America Country Music Association International's Hall of Fame. As a writer, her most coveted awards, in addition to the Robert J. Burton Award that she won for "Most Performed Song of the Year," are her Million-Air Awards, presented to writers of songs that achieve the blockbuster status of one million or more performances. In 2009, the state of North Carolina named a highway after her, and in 2010, she was inducted into the North Carolina Music Hall of Fame.

Prior to achieving superstardom and becoming one of the most prolific songwriters in Nashville, Donna was a high school English teacher. It was her love of the English language and her desire to communicate sincere and honest emotions that compelled Donna to try her hand at writing something other than song lyrics. Donna is also the author of *My Prayer for You, My Friend,* and her writings appear on Blue Mountain Arts greeting cards, calendars, and other gift items.

A Note from Donna

The writings in this book came along before I experienced the loss of my wonderful husband, so now I must search for the meaning of my life without him. I will always believe that everything is possible with God, but I know now that not everything is guaranteed.

Stan was everything to me. We completed each other. He taught me to play guitar and inspired my love songs. He was the publisher of the songs I wrote, and he produced all of our hit records in addition to the songs I recorded by other writers. Fans of my music know the titles, which space does not allow us to list here. Stan managed everything — from the decisions with the various companies I recorded for to the road shows with the band and singers, the touring events in this country and other countries, my TV show and other TV and Vegas engagements, and my rewarding writing career with Blue Mountain Arts.

Because our love, lives, and careers were so intertwined, his loss is beyond anything I will ever find words for... but I can say with certainty that there really is such a thing as true love, and he and I were so blessed to share it. I remind myself that God is our Creator and we belong to Him, so we are subject to His will and way. We serve an awesome God. I must surrender now to His sovereignty and supernatural wisdom and allow love and faith to sustain me and lead me the rest of the way — knowing that Stan's body may be gone, but our love will never die.

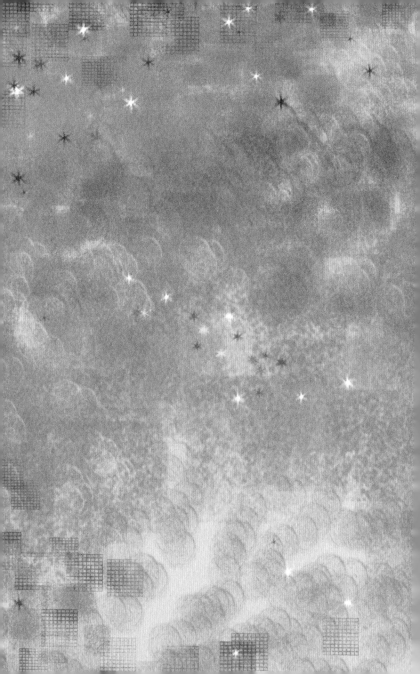